SOLÈNE ANGLARET

Where?

Published in Australia by
BeBeyondBorders
Elsternwick, VIC 3185
Tel: 0478692529
Email: bebeyondborders@yahoo.com
Website: www.bebeyondborders.com

First published in Australia 2019
Copyright © Solène Anglaret 2019

All rights reserved. No part of this publication may be reproduced, stored in a retrieval system, or transmitted, in any form or by any means without the prior written permission of the publisher, nor be otherwise circulated in any form of binding or cover other than that in which it is published and without a similar condition being imposed on the subsequent purchaser.

A catalogue record for this book is available from the National Library of Australia

Anglaret, Solène
WHERE?

ISBN: 978-0-6482432-3-6 (paperback)
ISBN: 978-0-6482432-4-3 (epub)

Cover layout and design by Christine Lugtu
Book typesetting by Christine Lugtu
Printed by IngramSpark®

Disclaimer
All care has been taken in the preparation of the information herein, but no responsibility can be accepted by the publisher or author for any damages resulting from the misinterpretation of this work. All contact details given in this book were current at the time of publication but are subject to change.

The advice given in this book is based on the experience of the individuals. Professionals should be consulted for individual problems. The author and publisher shall not be responsible for any person with regard to any loss or damage caused directly or indirectly by the information in this book.

To all the Dreamers
Beyond Borders,

And to poetry ...

A parallel universe
A sanctuary
A home

Where the deepest
And rawest wounds
Mysteriously heal

Contents

Preface 6

Chapter 1: Where from? 15

Chapter 2: Where now? 43

Chapter 3: Where to? 67

Parting thoughts 92

Acknowledgements 98

About the author 99

Preface

From

Find your place
Buy your ticket
Buckle your belt

For this ride ahead will take you ...

From safety
To uncertainty

From obvious
To mysterious

From there
To everywhere

Me

Did you call me pretty?
Ghosts of the past said I was ugly.

Did you consider me bright?
Inner voice sighed "that can't be right."

Did you really know me?

Passionate storyteller
Dedicated believer
Professional dreamer

In your eyes, I looked for an answer.
In your arms, I felt my guard lower.

Aspiring artist
Tenacious idealist
Wannabe optimist

Of myself, I could never be an analyst.
To this day, my rooted doubts persist.

Explorer
Traveller
Globetrotter

On the road, I looked for a deeper meaning.
On my own, I hoped for a new beginning.

Curious
Oblivious
Ambiguous

I kept changing with the seasons
And found even trickier questions ...

Who was I?
Who am I?
Who will I be?

Envious of those who know themselves
How would I ever describe myself?

As a lover of humanity
As an advocate of diversity
As a simple short story

The search continues slow and steady
My mind, my heart, my soul so messy

Impatient
Distant
Irreverent

Perhaps to your version of me I should stick
Or better still, my own path I shall finally pick.

> If only ...
> It felt easy
> To be me

To

A to B
A to Z

Paths we take
Choices we make

Am I in control?
Is fate on a roll?

I wish I knew.

Do you have any clue?
Why we do what we do?

You to Me
Me to You

You

Mysterious reader
Hiding undercover
One day supportive,
The next destructive.

Observing me hiding in the darkness
Judging me, inquisitive and relentless

Be warned!

Somewhere within this prose
My whole being I shall expose

CHAPTER ONE

Where from?

Was

I was young
I was strong

Bold, naive, and trusting,
For a home, I started looking.

No inhibitions
No limitations

Bubbly, fun, and caring,
Around the world, I started travelling.

I was limitless
I was fearless

Little, cute, and loving,
Diversity, I started embracing.

No barriers
No frontiers

I was it all.
But *who* was I?

Tough

At the ceiling I stare
Yet another nightmare

Inner voice screaming
Tight heart pounding

Not pretty enough!
Not smart enough!
Not funny enough!
Not good enough!

Never being enough
Isn't it tough?

Tougher

Feeling so alone
Chilled to the bone

I shouldn't talk to myself this way
Please send these demons away

All I ask for is sleep
Sweet, calm and deep
Forget about reality
Play a soothing melody

But there is no escape
And so, I lie awake

Silently hoping that later
Won't rhyme with tougher

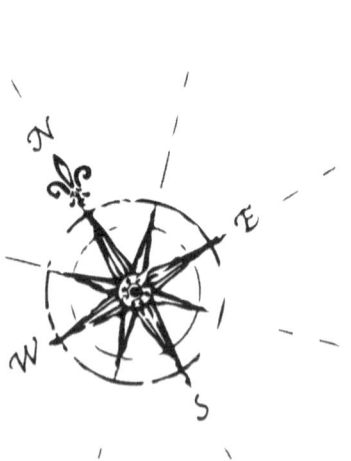

Home is ...

Wherever you find

Family

Family

From Asia to Australia
From Africa to America

My parents, my sister, and I together

Above and beyond the distance
And the burden of their absence

Neither words of poetry
Nor pompous liturgy
Have enough profundity
To describe our unity

Though we never say a thing
Our bond means everything

The fact that it remains silent
Doesn't mean it isn't decadent

My parents, my sister, and I together

As the years slowly roll by
As all shed tears eventually dry

No need to state the obvious
To our love no one is oblivious

From Normandy
One and only family
Forever and unconditionally
Praying for each other's immortality

Friends

Two peas in a pod
Inseparable

Then one day silence
Inexplicable

What happened, I have no clue
Every day is a darker shade of blue

Seven years later
An apology

Two peas reunited
Awkwardly

I can't believe my ears
My eyes fill with tears

We smile at each other
Once again us together

Same but somewhat different –
Older, wiser, and more patient

Words come flooding out
So much to talk about

May we be friends ...
Again?

International

When I was young and free,
I loved writing poetry.

As the years went by,
Words waved goodbye.

The two languages I spoke,
Became something bespoke.

They left me totally bemused ...
Family and friends confused.

English

What to write?
Is that right?

Losing my mother tongue ...

Quand j'étais jeune et bohème,
J'aimais écrire des poèmes.

Des mois et des années ont passé,
Les mots se sont envolés.

De deux langues maîtrisées,
A un tout mélangé.

Elles m'ont laissé perdue …
Famille et amis confus.

Français

Qu'écrire ?
Et que dire ?

Perdre ma langue maternelle…

Some call me bilingual.
Others say bye-lingual.

In summary,
International
Is what defines me,
And who I'll forever be.

Certain me disent bilingue.
D'autres un peu dingue.

En résumé,
Internationale
Est-ce ce que je suis,
Hier, demain et aujourd'hui

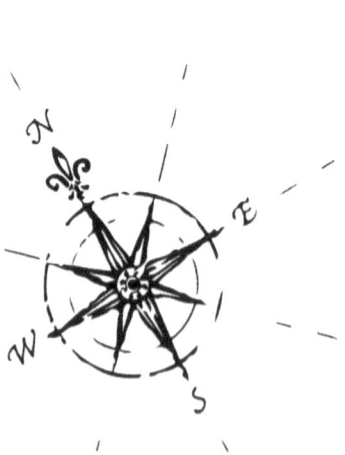

Home is ...

The love between

You and me

Days

Sun shining
People smiling
Hearts warming

He says

Keep writing
Keep creating
Keep dreaming

Music plays

Drums beating
Rhythm shifting
Melody lifting

Wait!

Softly in my ear, he says
As the music loudly plays
Here's to the good days

Dreams

Dive into colourful skies
Drop your baskets of lies

Reflect on what has been
Rewrite where we begin

Escape if you're sick and tired
Explode when I get you fired

Admit that we're intense
Accept not to make sense

Murmur secrets in my ear
Move your warm body near

Sweep me off my feet
Sweet dreams of heat

Seduced

You lured me into obeying you
You tricked me into loving you
You begged me to please you
You forced me to believe you

Your arguments baffled me
Your affection confused me
Your embrace distracted me
Your words forever scarred me

My values forgotten
My laughter silenced
My personality erased
My purpose ignored

I followed your lead
I followed your path
I was seduced
I was reduced

To being yours

Yours only
Yours sadly

Not yours truly

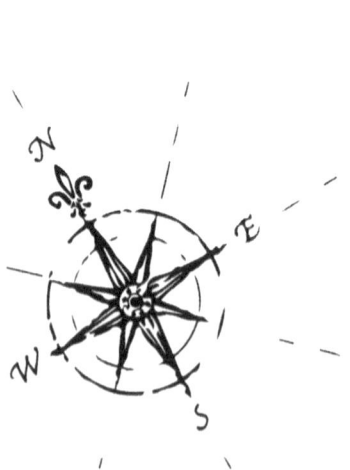

Home is ...

Where you can ugly cry

Shamelessly

Forever

Shadows moving along
Silences becoming long

I whispered 'I love you'
You replied 'Me too'

Early the next day
You left me anyway

Now it is with your ghost
That I hang out the most

Not exactly what I wished for
When I begged you for more

Who knew that by forever
You actually meant never

Rain

That day the rain
Like drops of pain

Quietly brushed my face

His sorry
Like pity
Too puny
For me

That day the rain
Like drops of pain

Slowly eroded my shame

Truth is ...
He was the one to blame

Doubts

Crippled by pity
Damaged by pain
Ambushed by memory
Tempted by gain

Wounded by life
Swallowed by shame
My inner voice a knife
Who was to blame?

Sly doubt
Kick it out

When reality strikes ...

Nowhere to hide
Nowhere to go

No one to listen
No one to help

No one to be
No one but me

CHAPTER TWO

Where now?

1

I am part
of a family

I am a member
of a community

I am a resident
of a city

I am a national
of a country

I am a detail
of a story

I am the dust
of a galaxy

I am one
of many

I am one
of me

Belong

Home is where I belong

Where is it?

It is a place
I long to find

What is it?

It is people
On my mind

Who is it?

It is a person
That is mine

Home belongs to me

Everywhere

Where are you from?
From everywhere.
Everywhere I have been
Been travelling and living
Living, breathing and loving
Loving my freedom
Freedom to move
Move all around
Around the world
World, our home
Home to millions
Millions and me
Me, you, and them too.

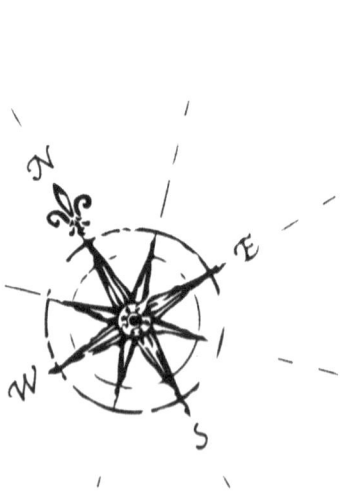

Home is ...

Wherever, Whatever, Whoever

You choose it to be

Homeless

They ask …
Why such travelling?
And such thinking?

They say …
You're homeless,
And hopeless.

They believe …
I'm a wanderer,
And a dreamer.

They call my life a fiction;
While ignoring my version.

I ask …
Why such intolerance?
And such resistance?

I say …
I'm 'homes full',
And hopeful.

I believe …
You and I could,
If only we would …

Live in total harmony,
Together peacefully.

Lonely

Darkness fills my dreams
Lonely, my heart screams

Slower
Lower
Emptier

Not an inch of me
Is who I wish to be

Life

When I'm upset, you're the one I blame
When I'm down, I call you lazy and lame

Like a project you have a beginning
Like a dream you have an ending

Apparently, I should trust you
Apparently, I must cherish you

If only you and I could be
Forever and after happy

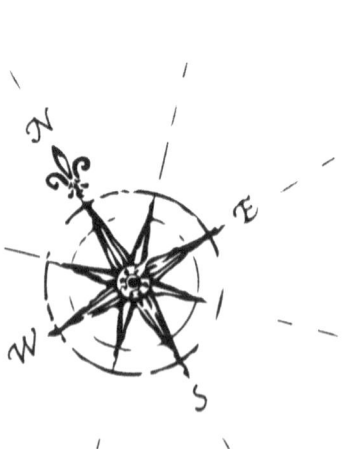

Home is ...

Where you can let go

Wholeheartedly

Despair

Is it all falling apart ...
Or just my work of art?
Of life I have learned a lesson
Of love I have made my mission.

Once lost, hopefully found
A path crossed, solid ground.

Some pray to an almighty God
Others isolate themselves in a pod.

Have you heard that yoga
Could align your chakra?
Or perhaps with meditation
You could find some elevation?

Not feeling spiritual today
My anger won't go away
Let me simmer on my own
Watch in silence as I drown

I've heard that from pain
All artists can gain.
I guess feeling like this
Predicts a masterpiece.

For another failure
For another fracture
Would be
For me

Too much to handle
Too late too little ...

Emptied of all hope
Despair and I could elope
In its arms safe and sound
The two of us are bound.

Missed

You thought
there was light.
It was a missed-take.

Too little

You thought
life would wait.
It was in vain.

Too late

You missed what
could have been.

You missed the
train of life.

You. Missed. It. All.

Recovery

Heavy rain began falling
Relentless and unforgiving

Only then, did I stop running
Only then, did I start thinking

Drop after drop pouring
Tear after tear dropping

Soaked and shaking
Why was I now smiling?

Doubts slowly disappearing
Deep regrets finally fading

The shower stopping
Left me staring

Water had changed something
Somehow diluted my suffering
There I was, slowly recovering

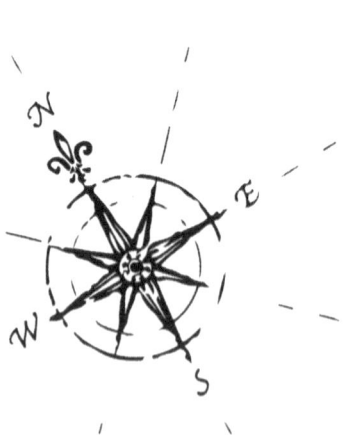

Home is ...

Somewhat of an escape

From reality

Us

You and me
Is like
Me and you

And

Him and her
Is like
Her and him

And

Him and him
Is like
Her and her

Why?

You
Me
Him
Her

Equals
One

Equals
Us

Them

The foreigners
The strangers

Those you don't know,
Those who don't show

Their pain
At your disdain.

Aliens to your nation,
Give me one good reason

Why only disparity you see?

Embracing our similarity
Isn't a denial of individuality.

It is painting without a frame
For we are part of them.

Together

I am sorry ...
Please tell me,
What is your worry?

Are you terrified of shame?
Are you avoiding the blame?

If you ask me
I don't believe therapy
Will make you healthy

Instead I recommend you travel
Explore the world and marvel
Get lost in wilderness and nature
Learn about every single culture

Your adventure complete
The two of us shall meet

For a brighter
New chapter
Together

CHAPTER THREE

Where to?

Message

Little bird at your window
Sitting there looking in

Too beautiful
To be discreet

Too cheerful
To be contained

Too truthful
To be silenced

Lush white feathers
Staring at your shadow

Waiting to be noticed
Before flying away

A tout jamais

Fly

Spread your wings wide
Take a chance and glide

Fly away
Your way

Away

Equality is a choice
Listen to our voice

One world
One people

Beyond nations
Above divisions

Working together
Sharing hope and laughter

May it happen in some way
Before death takes me away

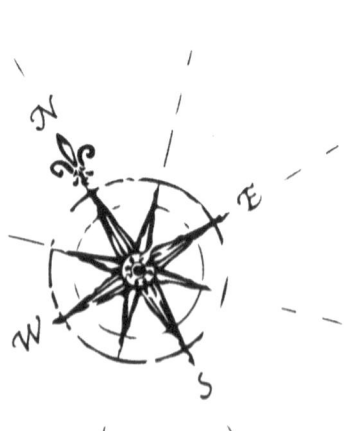

Home is ...

When you allow yourself

To just be

Survival

Left
Right

Escape your prison in a fight
Walk towards the horizon so bright

Fast
Forward

Turn your back on excruciating pain
Free your mind from its strangulating chain

Deep
Down

Aim for the moon
Break out of your cocoon

In
Out

Take a breath
Embrace the depth

Right
Left

Borders

Before she realised it
You placed her in a box
And locked it.

But it is far beyond
That her and I belong

The borders of your mind
Have made you blind

Powered by ignorance
Consumed by intolerance
You missed the evidence

That there is only one world
That there is only one people
That there is only one dream

Embracing both our differences and similarities
Living together peacefully and free
Being beyond borders

World

Haven't you had enough?
Said the world

Aren't you worn?
Aren't you bored?
Aren't you lonely?
Aren't you gloomy?
Echoed the ocean

Why do you keep moving?
Why do you keep travelling?
Why do you keep getting up?
Why do you keep reaching up?
Whispered the trees

You should stop wondering!
You should stop wandering!
You should give in!
You should stay in!
Insisted the wind

But why would I?

I am not gloomy
Moving gives me energy
I am not lonely
Travelling sets me free

And when I settle
Even just for a little

For a minute I am happy
But sadly, being me
I soon dream to flee
To the challenge of a new city

World, I will never have enough
As although it has been tough
You've always been home to me
And that's where I'd rather be

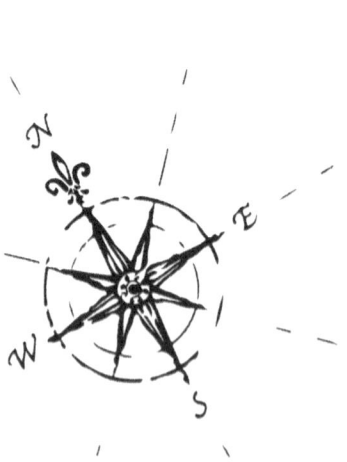

Home is ...

The whole world

Around me

Globetrotter

Packing and unpacking
Welcome to my routine!

Me, my monster bag and I
A little bit scared, I won't lie ...

But I know that's only the start
Travelling the world is an art

A tango with bravery
With adventure, a party

I've heard some say
That I'm running away

But I know that this passionate dance
Isn't a meaningless summer romance

The curious explorer in me
Wouldn't live any differently

Discovery after discovery
Both my feet endlessly itchy

Take me to new places there
To meet people everywhere

For as long as I'm healthy,
A globetrotter I shall be

Galaxy

"Where have you been?"
You enquired.

Here ... there ... everywhere ...
I answered.

"What is that supposed to mean?"

Well, the question should be:
Where *haven't* I been?

"And did that make you happy?"
You asked judgingly.

To go to every country,
In the entire galaxy,
Didn't only make me happy –

It made me free.
It made me, *me*.

Legacy

Out of hundreds, how many countries will I see?
It depends on how long I stay fit and healthy
All of them, three times over, if it were up to me

First time curious
Second time local
Third time lucky

Sadly, a lifetime won't be enough, nor will the money
I won't stop travelling and moving despite that reality
Being Beyond Borders is now second nature to me

For my message
For my life
And my story

Shall be my legacy

Home is ...

Who knows

Really?

Gratitude

Today you're there
Warming me up
Under your gaze

Looking at you
My eyes squint
Gently, I smile

Ray after ray
You remind me
To be grateful

For whatever time
I will have left
To see you shine

Future

If truth be told,
I have no idea
What the future will hold

"You won't know"
Whispers the wind
In a voice deep and slow

Fate shall play its curious part

Trust the uncertainty
And await your destiny

Step-by-step, dance and …
Arm yourself with patience

For one day will be your last
And all of life will be your past

Next

What comes after
The end of the text
Will be banter
About what comes next

Because for all we know
What the future has in store
Might be plenty of sorrow
Floods of tears and more

In a pile of dust
We shall disappear
Unless you trust
For heaven to appear

In the meantime, let it be
And strive to die happy!

Parting thoughts

Goodbye

One minute you were near
Your laughter all I could hear
Next thing I know
Far away you go

A tight embrace seals our goodbye
A nonchalant kiss as you drive by
My heart helplessly torn
An immense void born

Thought I was independent and strong
Seems as though I had it all wrong
You made me weak to my knees
My brain suddenly filled with bees

With the overwhelming noise
Long forgotten is my poise
Sobbing alone in the street
Feeling miserable and bleak

All that's in my power
For life not to seem dire
Is think about seeing you again
For my heart a soothing aim

To walk in sync together
And smile at each other
To hold your hand in mine tightly
And stare into your eyes intensely

To share a meal with you
And order a room for two
Please, just a little longer,
To myself I softly whisper

Maybe one day I will tell you
How much I truly miss you

But the entire alphabet
Wouldn't be long enough
The sound of a trumpet
Wouldn't be loud enough
To say what I wish I could

If only my pride would
Let me speak out
And tell you about
How my heart skips a million beats
As your breath brushes my cheeks

My love for you spreads beyond
The lands to which we belong
May what we have never get old
Even if we both become bold

May either close or far away
We end up together anyway

May years slowly pass by
Before our final goodbye

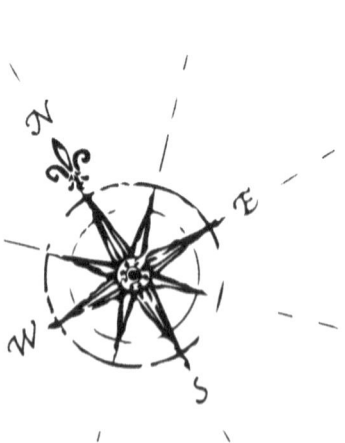

Home is ...

You tell

Me

Acknowledgements

This collection was written over the course of a year somewhere between Australia, Laos, Vietnam, France, and the United Kingdom. It is a project very dear to my heart that wouldn't have been possible without the support and guidance of two brilliant editors: Julie Richards and Sally-Anne Watson Kane, and the beautiful work of graphic designer Christine Lugtu. I would like to also take this opportunity to thank Leo Taylor and Matt Howden for being such helpful early readers. Grateful isn't a strong enough word to describe how I feel towards my dear sister Anaïs and my wonderful parents Alice and Philippe Anglaret. Finally, a huge thank you to my fiancé Andrew Small for reading through these pages more times than either of us can remember.

Keen to find out more about Solène?

www.bebeyondborders.com
bebeyondborders@yahoo.com
@bebeyondborders

About the Author

Solène was only a little girl when she started playing with words. In her teens, poetry became an outlet for her anger as well as a way to express her deepest fears and desires. She carefully transcribed all her favourite poems into a little book that can still be found in her home town of Louviers. Solène was only 18 when she moved abroad alone for the first time. Since then, she has lived in six countries (France, Norway, the United States, the United Kingdom, China and now Australia) and has visited more than 50. Through her travels, Solène became what some might call bilingual or, more accurately, 'bye-lingual'. It is only recently that she regained enough confidence and started writing again. *Where?* is her third publication after her travel memoir *Where to Next?* and her children's story *Where Are You From?* With all her writing, Solène explores the concepts of home and sense of belonging. Ultimately, she aspires to contribute to making the world a place of tolerance, acceptance, and peace.

www.ingramcontent.com/pod-product-compliance
Lightning Source LLC
Chambersburg PA
CBHW032046290426
44110CB00012B/972